# HOW TO REPRESENT YOURSELF IN SMALL CLAIMS COURT AND WIN

*A step by step guide for plaintiffs and defendants*

Jay Barr

(c) 2019, Do It Yourself Legal Guides. All rights reserved. This guide and any portion thereof may only be used by the person it was purchased for. Republishing, sharing, or otherwise reproducing any portion of this guide for any other use is strictly prohibited, except as expressly authorized by Federal law, the author, and/or the publisher.

# CONTENTS

Chapter 1: Introduction to Small Claims Court ............................................................. 5
    Key Points About the civil legal system and Small Claims Court ..................... 8
    Steps in a Small Claims Case ............................................................................10
    Glossary of Terms ............................................................................................. 11

Chapter 2: Filing a small Claim .....................................................................................18
    Step One: Filing A Small Claim.........................................................................18
    Step Two: The Defendant's Answer or Filing for Default................................ 24

CHAPTER 3: Serving the small claim and other legal documents ........................ 27
    How to Find the Defendant .............................................................................. 27
    How to Serve the Small claim notice .............................................................. 29

Chapter 4: Defending Against A Small Claims Lawsuit............................................. 32
    Debt Collection Lawsuits ................................................................................. 34

Chapter 5: How to Find, Prepare, and ........................................................................37
Introduce Evidence .........................................................................................................37
    Procuring Witnesses ........................................................................................ 38
    Procuring Exhibits: .......................................................................................... 43

chapter 6: At the small claims Hearing...................................................................... 48
    Mediation.......................................................................................................... 48
    Steps at the Hearing ........................................................................................ 50
    Examining Witnesses....................................................................................... 53
    Objections ........................................................................................................ 54

CHAPTER 7: How to Collect on A Judgment............................................................... 59
    Garnishing Bank Accounts .............................................................................. 60

    Garnishing Wages..................................................................................63
CONCLUSION ........................................................................................65
APPENDIX 1: Sample Pleadings.......................................................... 66
appendix 2: Glossary............................................................................75

# CHAPTER 1: INTRODUCTION TO SMALL CLAIMS COURT

Thank you for purchasing 'How to Represent Yourself in Small Claims Court and Win' from Do It Yourself Legal Guides! If you have purchased this guide, then you are either considering filing a civil lawsuit in small claims court or someone has filed a small claims lawsuit against you. Either way, this guide provides a detailed overview of the small claims process in the United States. Although the specific details of filing a small claim will vary from state to state, this instructions in this guide will definitely be useful in your particular jurisdiction. It will tell you everything you need to know about filing or defending against a small claim, including:

1. How to properly draft and serve a small claim complaint;
2. How to file and serve an answer to a small claim complaint;
3. What type of evidence you will need to prosecute or defend against a small claim in front of a judge (and how to obtain it);
4. How to introduce evidence, question witnesses, and offer objections at the small claims hearing;
5. How to collect any money you are awarded at the hearing.

Each chapter of this guide is presented in a chronological, easy to follow order. This guide also contains sample images of some documents in Appendix 1. Although these documents are specific to one jurisdiction (in this case, Oregon), referring to them will be very helpful when you are drafting your own documents.

Before we dive into the details of small claim procedures, here are a few key points to keep in mind:

- Every state has a small claims court system, designed to expedite small legal disputes and keep costs down for both plaintiffs and defendants. The dollar amount of a legal dispute usually governs whether or not a claim can be brought in small claims court. In Oregon, the maximum amount of a small claim is $10,000. In Colorado, it is $7,500, and in New York it is $5,000. If you want to sue someone for more than the maximum amount, you will need to file your case in regular trial court. Do it Yourself Legal Guides also publishes a civil litigation guide that outlines the general procedure for civil trial court. Although some of the information is the same as in this guide, it will no doubt prove useful if your case is not heard in small claims court.
- Although small claims courts generally follow the same legal principals as a regular trial court, the rules of procedure are much more relaxed. A judge hearing a small claims case will not expect the parties to be familiar with the details of evidentiary rules or civil procedure. That said, you must still present credible evidence that proves each element of your claim or defense.
- This guide contains everything you will need to exercise your legal rights in small claims court from start to finish. All of our guides are created by licensed attorneys with years of

experience. While it is impossible to predict every single course of action your case may take, this guide will give you the knowledge you need to confidently adjust to any situation you may find yourself in during the course of small claims litigation.

- This guide is intentionally written in an easy to understand format. It endeavors to avoid legal jargon and simplify the issues whenever possible. For example, when discussing serving legal documents, this guide details the most common service methods, without discussing every possible way to serve a party. On a similar note, there may very well be narrow exceptions to many of the instructions given in this guide that are not mentioned. The purpose of this guide is to offer an easy to understand process for navigating the small claims system, rather than offering a detailed review of every possible scenario.

- Although attorneys are generally not allowed to represent parties in small claims court, they can advise parties on any and all matters before the hearing. If you can afford to consult with an attorney, it never hurts to do so.

- That said, legal jargon and obtuse rules often make the legal process seem much more complicated than it really is. Law is not rocket science or brain surgery and you will be surprised at just how much of the legal field is based on simple, common-sense theories, even when the rules seem to be written in a different language. With this guide you will be able to navigate this needlessly complicated arena with confidence.

# KEY POINTS ABOUT THE CIVIL LEGAL SYSTEM AND SMALL CLAIMS COURT

If you are (or might become) a plaintiff or defendant in a small claims lawsuit, you should be familiar with the basics of how the civil legal system works:

- Almost every civil lawsuit in any state is filed in that state's trial court system. These courts are usually organized by county. The exact name of this court will vary from state to state. For example, in Oregon the trial court system is referred to as Oregon Circuit Court, in California it is called California Superior Court, and in Texas, it is referred to as Texas District Court.
- The federal government also has their own court system, referred to as United States District Court, where issues of federal law are usually decided. However, any small claims case will definitely be heard in state court.
- Every state has hundreds of laws (often referred to as 'statutes') on the books, which will all have similar, but slightly different names, such as the Oregon Revised Statutes or California Code. In addition to statutes, states will have specific rules of civil procedure that all courts must follow. They will also have trial court rules that further detail the procedures that govern civil actions.
- In order to track down all these laws and rules in your state, keep in mind the following:

- Statutes are created by the state legislature and you will easily be able to find the official codes online by going to your state legislature's website. The rules of civil procedure should also be available at the state level.
- To find out about your trial court rules, contact the specific courthouse your case is (or will be) heard in.
- Although this may sound daunting, do not be intimidated! You will not need to read every statute and rule of civil procedure in order to competently represent yourself. In fact, once you know the specific legal issue you need to look into, you will easily be able to find the relevant information, whether it is a statute, state-wide trial court rule, or a local rule.
- In addition to reviewing statutes online, your local law library will be a great resource for more in-depth research. Check with your particular county court to find out the hours and location of your local law library.
- Generally speaking, a claim made in small claims court needs to be proven by a PREPONDERANCE OF THE EVIDENCE, which simply means that the claims made by the plaintiff must be 'more likely than not' to have occurred. The burden of proof is always on the plaintiff. They need to introduce evidence related to each element of their claim that will show the judge it is 'more likely than not' to be the truth. If the plaintiff fails to do so, the defendant will win the case, regardless of whether or not they put on any kind of defense.
- One of the best ways to learn about the small claims process is to go to the courthouse and watch a few small claims hearings. Contact the calendaring department of your local courthouse and find out when small claims hearings are being held. These proceedings are open to the public and anyone can attend. Just

make sure you are quiet and respectful when watching any court proceeding.

## STEPS IN A SMALL CLAIMS CASE

Generally, all small claim lawsuits contain the following steps (which will be discussed in greater detail throughout this guide):

1. A SMALL CLAIM NOTICE or COMPLAINT is filed by the PLAINTIFF at the courthouse. Regardless of the exact title, this is the basic claim wherein the plaintiff alleges how they have been harmed by the DEFENDANT.
2. The small claim notice is then served on the defendant, usually with a response form.
3. The defendant then has a certain number of days to file their response (in Oregon, for example, a defendant has 14 days to file the response after being served). In the response, the defendant can usually pay the claim, deny the claim and request a hearing before a judge, or sometimes request a jury trial in regular trial court.
4. If a response is filed that requests a small claims hearing, a hearing will be held in a few weeks.
5. Many states require the parties to attend a mediation session at the courthouse in an effort to resolve the situation without a formal hearing. If mediation is required, a date and time for mediation will be set before the hearing.
6. At the hearing, both sides will present their case and the judge will make a decision based on the evidence presented.

That's it! That's all there is to the small claims process. Of course, the details can get a bit more complicated, but this is the course almost every single small claim will take. If this process makes sense to you, you will be able to follow the rest of this guide with ease!

# GLOSSARY OF TERMS

The following glossary contains definitions of some of the most common legal terms you are likely to encounter in small claims court. You should review the glossary now before proceeding. Keep in mind that some of the terms below might not be relevant to your particular case. Also, note that the definitions in this glossary reflect how the terms are used in this guide in relation to civil court/small claims proceedings. Other legal definitions of the same terms may vary slightly or be somewhat more detailed. The glossary below is grouped in an easy to follow, non-alphabetical order that reflects how a case would generally proceed. An alphabetical glossary is included in Appendix 2.

**In the Beginning:**

**PARTY:** A plaintiff or defendant in a civil case.
**PLAINTIFF:** A person who files a civil lawsuit against a defendant.
**DEFENDANT:** A person who has been accused of wrongdoing by a plaintiff in civil court.
**PRO SE:** Latin phrase meaning, "for oneself". It refers to any plaintiff or defendant that does not have an attorney. They are referred to as a *pro se* litigant or proceeding *pro se*.

**CONTRACT LAW:** One of two broad categories of civil lawsuits. All legal issues dealing with any written or oral agreement will be based on contract law.

**TORT LAW:** The other broad category of civil lawsuits that basically includes any type of wrongful act committed by another (other than breach of contract cases), such as battery or negligence.

**PLEADINGS:** Any formal document that is filed with the court in a civil case.

**COMPLAINT:** The initial document filed by a plaintiff that begins a civil lawsuit in circuit court (referred to as a 'small claim', 'notice of small claim', or something similar in small claims court). It is a statement of how the plaintiff has been wronged by the defendant and why they should be compensated. It includes one or more claims for relief and alleges how each element of that claim has been satisfied.

**CLAIM FOR RELIEF:** A specific cause of action alleged in a complaint, such as a claim of negligence or a claim of racial discrimination.

**ELEMENT:** A specific aspect of a claim that must be properly alleged (and ultimately proven) to prevail on a claim for relief. A claim will normally have several elements, each of which must be proven by a preponderance of the evidence.

**RESPONSE:** The formal reply to a small claim notice, filed by the defendant (referred to as an 'Answer' in regular circuit court). A response will usually deny the claims and either request a hearing or a jury trial.

**AFFIRMATIVE DEFENSE:** A type of defense asserted in a response in which, even if the allegations in the plaintiff's small claim are true (i.e. affirmed), the plaintiff is still not entitled to relief. For example, if the allegations in the small claim are true, but the statute of limitations has expired, the defendant would assert the affirmative defense of failing to bring a claim within the statutory period.

**STATUTE OF LIMITATIONS:** A period set by law in which a claim for relief must be filed. For example, if the statute of limitations on a personal injury (negligence) case is two years, the plaintiff would need to file a claim for negligence within two years of the date they discovered the injury.

**CONTRACT:** Any agreement (oral or written), in which an offer has been made by one party, accepted by another, and some consideration has been given (such as money, or performance of a specific task). Breach of contract is one of the most commonly filed civil claims (whether in small claims court or regular circuit court).

**Procedural Issues:**

**STATUTES:** The codified laws of a state. The official name of these statutes will vary from state to state.

**RULES OF CIVIL PROCEDURE:** The basic rules of civil court proceedings. Each state will have their own set of civil procedure rules (the official name of these rules will vary from state to state). These rules may or may not apply in small claims court.

**TRIAL COURT RULES:** More specific rules of a state that govern courtroom procedure which all county courts must follow (although all of these rules may not apply to small claims cases). The official name of these rules will vary from state to state.

**SMALL CLAIMS COURT:** A division of a state court that handles claims of low economic value (the exact amount varies by state). In most states, attorneys are not allowed to represent parties in small
claims court. It is intended to be a less formal and more cost-effective venue for resolving civil

disputes.

**SERVICE:** The term that refers to the specific notice that pleadings have been received by an opposing party.

**PROCESS SERVER:** A person who is hired by a party to deliver legal documents to someone in accordance with the rules of civil procedure.

**CERTIFICATE OF SERVICE:** A document filed with the court (signed by the process server) showing that service has been completed in accordance with the rules of civil procedure.

**MOTION:** Any formal request by a party, asking the court to take a certain course of action.

**DEFAULT JUDGMENT:** A judgment entered against a defendant who has failed to appear after being properly served with a summons and complaint or a small claim notice.

**MEDIATION:** A formal meeting between the parties and a neutral mediator in which the mediator attempts to broker a settlement that is agreeable to both sides. Unlike an arbitrator, the mediator does not have any authority to issue a decision in favor of one party. Their only purpose is to negotiate with both parties and attempt to craft a mutually agreeable settlement. In many states, parties in a small claims case must attend a mandatory mediation session and work towards resolving the issue in good faith before proceeding to a hearing.

**ARBITRATION:** A less formal, but usually binding proceeding in which a civil dispute is resolved by a private arbitrator, rather than a judge. Arbitration is unlikely to be an issue in a small claims case.

**CONTEMPT OF COURT:** The offense of disobeying a court order. A judge can find a person in contempt and impose sanctions (usually a fine or other civil penalty, but on rare occasions it can include incarceration).

**HEARING:** A proceeding before a judge in which evidence is presented and a decision is made. The decision at a hearing may affect one aspect of a case, or it may resolve the case entirely, depending on the nature of the specific hearing.

**TRIAL:** A proceeding in which a final decision is made based on the merits of a case. A hearing where evidence is presented and a judge or jury finds in favor of the plaintiff or defendant.

**BENCH TRIAL:** A trial in which there is no jury. The judge will decide all issues of law and fact. All small claims hearings are heard by a judge.

**JURY TRIAL:** A trial in which a jury decides all factual issues. A judge will preside over the case and decide all legal issues, but the final decision regarding liability and damages will be made by the jury.

**DISMISSAL WITHOUT PREJUDICE:** The dismissal of a plaintiff's case wherein they can refile their complaint. In other words, a judge thought the case had serious flaws, but the flaws could potentially be resolved and the case could still be refiled if the deficiencies are corrected.

**DISMISSAL WITH PREJUDICE:** The dismissal of a plaintiff's case, wherein the plaintiff cannot refile against the defendant regarding the same issue. The judge has decided that the problems with the case are so great, they cannot possibly be corrected.

**JUDGMENT CREDITOR:** A person who has been awarded monetary damages in a civil lawsuit.

**JUDGMENT DEBTOR:** A person who has been ordered to pay a monetary damage award in a civil lawsuit.

**APPEAL:** A request for a higher court to review the decision of a lower court. Appeals are usually not allowed in small claims cases.

**GARNISHMENT:** The legal seizing of another person's property (such as wages or funds in a bank account). Garnishment is often instituted to collect money awarded in a judgment.

**Evidence and Discovery:**

**EVIDENCE:** Anything that is submitted in a court proceeding to prove or disprove any claim or defense. Evidence includes (but is not limited to) oral testimony of witnesses, documents, video recordings, and material objects.
**DISCOVERY:** The stage of a civil lawsuit wherein both parties are obligated to turn over any potential evidence that is relevant to a claim or defense.
**PREJUDICIAL:** In this context, prejudicial refers to how *unfairly* harmful a piece of evidence is. Evidence that would not be excluded for any other reason, can still be excluded if it will unfairly bias a jury. For example, if the jury knows a party has been convicted of a crime unrelated to the issue at hand, that could unfairly skew their impression of the party. They could seek to have that fact excluded as having more prejudicial than probative value (although there are exceptions to this particular scenario).
**PROBATIVE:** A term used to describe how strong a piece of evidence is in regards to its ability to help prove or disprove any claim or defense. How probative a piece of evidence is will often be a factor in whether or not it is admitted into the record. Evidence that has no probative value will likely be excluded.
**DEPOSITION:** A formal interview of a witness that is recorded (usually by a court reporter transcribing the deposition).
**DEPONENT:** The witness who is being deposed.

**WITNESS:** Any person that provides testimony in a court proceeding. They can be a party to the litigation or any other person.

**SUBPOENA:** A command by a court or attorney requiring a person to appear for a deposition or hearing/trial.

**SUBPOENA DUCES TECUM:** A command by a court or attorney requiring a person to produce specific documents or other material objects.

**EXHIBIT:** Any piece of evidence (other than witness testimony) that is submitted for review by a judge or jury, whether at trial or pursuant to a motion, deposition or other hearing.

**OBJECTION:** A formal protest by one party to the actions of the other party. For example, if a party seeks to submit evidence that is not in accordance with a state's rules of evidence, a party might object to its entry on the grounds that it fails to comply with said rule.

Now that you have an understanding of the basics of the civil court system and small claim process, we can proceed to Chapter 2, wherein you will learn how to properly prepare and file a small claim.

# CHAPTER 2: FILING A SMALL CLAIM

Small claims court is one of the easiest and fastest ways for a person to seek relief via the judicial system. The process in small claims court is much simpler than filing a claim in a state's regular trial court. In fact, attorneys are (usually) not even allowed to represent plaintiffs or defendants if the case is heard in small claims court. That said, it is still vital that plaintiffs and defendants are prepared and well informed on how the small claims process works. Following the advice in this guide will give you a huge advantage over other non-represented parties and help you obtain a ruling in your favor.

## STEP ONE: FILING A SMALL CLAIM

The first step in filing a small claims case is for the plaintiff to obtain a small claim notice form from their local county courthouse (remember, the exact name of this document may vary, but if you tell the court you want to file a small claims case, they will almost certain have forms available). This is the initiating document for a small claims case, wherein the plaintiff describes how they have been harmed by the defendant. Unlike trial court, there are not really any hard and fast rules a person needs to abide by when writing out their claim. A plaintiff only needs to assert that they were somehow harmed by the defendant and they should be ordered to compensate the plaintiff for that harm. The judge will make their decision with the goal of resolving the issue in the most equitable manner possible.

In the main body of the document, the plaintiff will need to explain to the court clearly and concisely how they have been harmed. Although they do not need to officially allege all the elements of a formal civil action (such as negligence or breach of contract), it is definitely helpful to do so if at all possible. While small claims judges are only required to make a decision that they feel is a fair resolution, they will certainly be using standard tort and contract law to guide them.

Before discussing common types of claims, both sides should be aware of the following:

- Be sure to check the statute of limitations on any claim that you want to file or that has been filed against you. If a plaintiff alleges a claim that is outside of the statute of limitations, their case will likely be dismissed. Most types of civil claims have a statute of limitations of at least one year, but two years is most common for a wide variety of civil claims. Breach of contract claims usually have a longer period such as 4, 6, or even 10 years. Statutes of limitations vary widely by state! If it has been a while since the events giving rise to a claim took place (especially if it has been over one year), it is imperative that the plaintiff checks the statute of limitations before filing!

- If a plaintiff is suing any type of government body in state court, they might have to file a tort claim notice before filing their lawsuit. Also, in some states, the time to file a tort claim notice is much shorter than the normal statute of limitations (although once the notice is filed, they will then have the rest of the statute of limitations period to file their claim).
- If a plaintiff is suing a contractor for work done on their home, they may have to give the contractor proper notice of their intent to file a lawsuit before actually filing a complaint. They may also need to file a claim with their state's board or agency that regulates contractors. Check with your state's contractor licensing authority for the correct procedure.
- If a plaintiff has a written contract with someone, they need to check the terms of the contract and make sure both sides have not agreed to a mandatory arbitration program. If they have, they will be required to go through that process instead of (or at least before) filing in small claims court. In that event, this guide will still be quite useful, as any such arbitration will involve discovery, evidence, and witness testimony, the processes of which will be based on state law.

After the plaintiff has reviewed the pre-filing requirements in their state and they feel they still have good cause, they should start drafting their claim. Samples of a completed small claim form from the State of Oregon are included in Appendix 1 of this guide, but keep in mind that the proper formatting will vary from state to state. Plaintiffs should review their state's trial court rules to find the proper formatting guidelines. It is always a good idea for both parties to make sure that their pleadings are professional looking and on par with what would be filed by an attorney. That said, if you are representing yourself, most courts will not be too concerned about whether or not you are in strict compliance with the formatting rules (also, if you are reading this guide in ebook format, be aware that the formatting of the samples will likely be somewhat skewed). As long as the complaint is easy to read and the claims are laid out clearly and concisely, the court clerk will almost certainly accept the pleading.

Some of the most common theories of recovery in small claims court and the standard elements of each (which may vary by state) are:

1. Breach of Contract. The plaintiff must allege and ultimately prove:
    a. Existence of a contract (either oral or written[1]), which includes an offer, acceptance, and some sort of consideration (such as money paid for a task performed).
    b. Breach of said contract by the defendant.
    c. Damages incurred.
2. Negligence. The plaintiff must allege and ultimately prove:
    a. The defendant's conduct caused the plaintiff harm;
    b. The risk of that harm was foreseeable;
    c. That defendant's conduct was unreasonable in light of the risk;
    d. The harm caused by the defendant resulted in the plaintiff incurring damages.
3. Battery. The plaintiff must allege and ultimately prove:
    a. The defendant intended to cause harmful or offensive physical contact;
    b. Such contact actually occurred;

---

[1] Contrary to popular belief, most oral contracts are enforceable. The specific terms of the contact are just harder to prove.

    c. The plaintiff suffered damages as a result of such contact.
4. Theft (called 'conversion' in legalese). The plaintiff must allege and ultimately prove:
    a. The defendant exercised dominion and control over the plaintiff's property to such an extent that the defendant should be ordered to return the property or pay the plaintiff its full value, in addition to compensating the plaintiff for loss of use of the property. If the loss of the property was only temporary and the plaintiff got it back, they can still claim damages for loss of use.

Below are 3 typical causes of action written in an acceptable small claims format, based on negligence, breach of contract, and theft/conversion:

**Example 1:**

"I, Plaintiff, claim that on or about 3/1/2017, I was shopping at ABC Supermarket, which is owned by Defendant[2]. While shopping, I slipped and fell on a puddle of water, injuring my back. Defendant has a duty to make sure his store is safe for people who shop there and by failing to keep the floors clean and dry, Defendant has failed in this duty. Defendant's actions have caused me $3,000 in damages, representing $1,500 in medical bills and $1,500 for pain, suffering, and inconvenience. Such amount is still due."

---

[2] A note on grammar: "The" is not normally used when referring to plaintiffs and defendants in actual pleadings. When referring to them generally, it is acceptable to use "the". You will see parties referred to in both ways throughout this guide. Also, as with all proper nouns, plaintiff and defendant should be capitalized when referring to a specific person, but not when using the terms in a general sense.

**Example 2:**

"I, Plaintiff, claim that on or about 12/09/2017, the above-named Defendant owed me the sum of $5,000 because I entered into an oral contract with Defendant to paint the outside of his house in exchange for $7,000. Defendant paid me $2000 up front, but failed to pay the remaining amount when I completed the job on 12/09/2017. Defendant has received the benefit of having a painted house, but has refused to pay the agreed upon price. Defendant's actions have damaged me in the amount of $5,000, and this amount is still due."

**Example 3:**

"I, Plaintiff, claim that on or about 9/1/2017, Defendant (who is my former roommate) stole my flat screen television and antique motorcycle when he moved out of my apartment. These were both purchased by me and have always been my property. Defendant had no right to take them. His actions have caused me damages in the amount of $6,000 representing $1,000 for the value of the television, $3,000 for the value of the motorcycle, and $2,000 for loss of use and pain/suffering/inconvenience. This amount is still due. In the alternative, Plaintiff requests that Defendant be ordered to return the property in the same condition as it was when it was wrongfully taken and award Plaintiff $2,000 in non-economic damages."

Whatever the facts of your particular case, be sure to lay them out very simply and inform the court how the defendant's actions have damaged you. If you can convince the judge that you were wronged in some way that caused you harm (either economic or non-economic) the judge will likely find in your favor, even if you do not allege a specific type of tort claim. Of course, you will only want to allege facts you can prove at the hearing (more on that later).

Once a plaintiff has properly alleged their claims, they will need to take the claim form to their county courthouse and file it with the court clerk. Most small claims filers prefer to file documents in person at the courthouse's civil filing window. However, parties may also be able to file their documents electronically online. If you would prefer to file online, check your court's website to see if this is an option in your jurisdiction.

Once the claim is filed and the filing fee has been paid, the plaintiff will need to serve a copy of their small claim on the defendant. The rules for service of a small claim are the same as they are for any other complaint (although a separate summons is usually not required). Refer to Chapter 3 for guidance on how to properly serve these documents on a defendant.

## STEP TWO: THE DEFENDANT'S ANSWER OR FILING FOR DEFAULT

If the defendant has been properly served, they will have a certain number of days from the date of service to file a response (how to properly respond to a small claim is discussed in Chapter 4). Generally, a defendant can usually: pay the claim or return the property (including paying the plaintiff's filing fee), request a hearing, file a counterclaim in small claims court, or possibly request a jury trial. Depending on how the defendant responds, the plaintiff's case will proceed as follows:

- If the defendant wants to pay the claim, your court will have instructions on how to go about doing so. It usually involves sending the money to the plaintiff directly, informing the court that they have paid the claim in full, and submitting proof of payment. It is also important to note that plaintiffs and defendants are free to negotiate settlement terms for less than the amount claimed. If this happens, both sides should be sure to get any such settlement in writing[3]. The plaintiff should then inform the court that the case has been settled and they would like to voluntarily dismiss their claim.
- If the defendant requests a hearing the case will proceed accordingly (see below).
- If the defendant files a counterclaim, the plaintiff will then have to respond to the claim, just as the defendant responded to the original claim. The case will then proceed and the plaintiff will have to prove their own claims while disproving the defendant's claims at the hearing.
- If the defendant requests a jury trial, the plaintiff will then have a certain amount of time to refile their claim as a civil complaint in the regular state trial court. If they fail to do so, the claim will be dismissed without prejudice (which means they can refile), but they will likely have to pay the defendant's filing fee in the small claim action.

If the defendant does not respond within the set time period, the plaintiff must seek a default judgment from the court. A default judgment is granted when the defendant has been properly served, but has failed to appear. The judge will take a quick look at the plaintiff's case to make sure service was proper and that their claim

---

[3] Such an agreement can be quite simple. Just state that the plaintiff agrees to dismiss their claim and not bring any other claims for the same actions against the defendant in exchange for them paying $XXXX to settle the claim.

is at least minimally reasonable on its face. The judge will then enter a judgment in the plaintiff's favor awarding them the damages claimed.

This is both good and bad news for the plaintiff. Good news in the sense that they will have won their case without having a full hearing. Bad in the sense that if the defendant did not show up, they will likely be difficult to track down and collecting on the judgment could be a problem.

The process for seeking a default judgment varies from state to state, but the basic principle is always the same. This usually takes the form of filing a 'motion for default', wherein the plaintiff proves to the court that the defendant was properly served and is aware of the pending lawsuit and has chosen not to file any kind of response by the set deadline. If a motion for default is filed, the court still may require the plaintiff to appear at the hearing and testify regarding the amount of damages they have claimed. Alternatively, they may simply sign an order and judgment granting the motion and awarding them the damages. Either way, so long as the defendant was properly served, the plaintiff will almost certainly win their case.

If the judge signs a default judgment, the plaintiff will now have an enforceable judgment that gives them the authority to collect what they are owed from the defendant. Refer to Chapter 7 for guidance on this step of the legal process. The next chapter discusses how to find and properly serve a defendant.

# CHAPTER 3: SERVING THE SMALL CLAIM AND OTHER LEGAL DOCUMENTS

Once the plaintiff has filed their small claim with the courthouse, they will need to serve it on the defendant. Rules regarding service are very specific and they must be followed precisely! Although there are a few different ways to serve a defendant, the best course of action is to have the claim served personally by an independent process server or your local sheriff. This way, there will be no doubt that the person was actually served (see below for more details on process servers).

## HOW TO FIND THE DEFENDANT

Ideally, the plaintiff will already know where the defendant resides or does business, so finding the proper address for service won't be a problem. If the plaintiff is having their process server serve the defendant personally, they might not even need their address (so long as they know where the defendant is going to be on any given day). If, however, the defendant's address is unknown, then the following resources will be helpful:

**Court Records:**

Most courthouses (or the nearest law library) will have a computer terminal where you can look up all civil and criminal records in the state. If the defendant has been sued before or has been charged with a crime, their address will likely be included in the court records. Just keep in mind that proper spelling is important, the address information may be outdated (especially if the only record is several years old), and there could very well be someone with the same name as the person you are looking for (try to use birthdate information to confirm, if you have that available).

**Motor Vehicle Records:**

Many state motor vehicle departments allow process servers and members of the public to access certain information. You may be able to obtain a defendant's address this way, but you will have to check with your state motor vehicle department to inquire about what information can be released.

**Business Records:**

All individuals and companies doing business in a state usually have to register with some sort of state agency. As part of this registration, they are usually required to list a 'Registered Agent', which is an entity or person that is designated to accept mail and legal documents on behalf of a business. For larger corporations, separate companies are used who do nothing but act as a registered agent for many different businesses. If you are suing a business, all legal documents should be sent to the registered agent, rather than the business's headquarters. Check your state's business registry for this information.

# HOW TO SERVE THE SMALL CLAIM NOTICE

Once the defendant's address is known, they can be served in a variety of ways. However, as mentioned above, personal service by a professional process server or the local sheriff is the best option. If you feel another method of service is appropriate for your case, you will need to check your state's rules of civil procedure for alternative methods of service.

**Personal Service:**

Personal service, as the name implies, means serving the defendant directly. It is usually the best course of action. Having a neutral, third-party serve a defendant directly greatly reduces the chance that the defendant will claim they were never served properly.

The best way to have a person/business served is to hire a professional process server. Of course, this is also the most expensive. The cost for such service is usually between $50-60. However, it is often worthwhile as this price will include a few attempts at one specific address and you can also rely on their professional expertise when it comes to making sure service is completed effectively. A simple internet search will give you a list of the process servers working in your geographical area.

The second-best option (and usually the second most expensive) is to pay a sheriff's deputy to serve the documents. Sheriff's departments in most states provide this service to the public for a fee.

If you do not want to incur the expense of hiring a professional process server, any adult of sound mind and body who is a resident of your state should be able to serve a defendant (but check your local rules of civil procedure!). You can even go with the person, so long as you are not the one who actually gives the documents to the defendant. The server simply needs to identify the defendant, inform the defendant that the server has some documents for him/her, and hand them over. That's it. You don't need to explain who you are or the nature of the documents.

If the person refuses to take them, simply inform them that it is really in their best interest to accept these documents and leave them at their feet (or on a counter/table/etc.).

**Filing the Proof of Service:**

Once service has been completed, the person who served the documents needs to sign a CERTIFICATE OF SERVICE, which is then filed with the courthouse to prove that the defendant has been made aware of the pending lawsuit. If a professional process server or the sheriff's department was used, they *should* fill out their own form and send it to the courthouse themselves (but follow up to make sure they do not forget). A sample of a completed certificate of service from the state of Oregon is included in Appendix 1.

Once service has been completed, the defendant will have a certain number of days from the date of service to file an answer to the small claim. If the defendant has not filed an answer or motion within the allotted time after being served, the plaintiff will need to petition the court for a default judgment, as discussed above.

**Serving Other Documents:**

Once the defendant has been served with the small claim notice, the rules regarding service of other legal documents for both parties are much more relaxed. Both parties will be required to list an address they can be served at in their initial pleadings. All future documents filed in the case can usually be mailed to that address via first class mail. Just remember to fill out a certificate of service for each group of documents you send going forward.

Chapter 4 discusses how a defendant should respond to a small claim. Once the defendant has been properly served and requested a hearing, both sides will need to begin preparing their witnesses and exhibits, which is the subject of Chapter 5.

# CHAPTER 4: DEFENDING AGAINST A SMALL CLAIMS LAWSUIT

When someone has been sued in small claims court, they will receive an official court pleading with a title similar to 'Small Claim' or 'Notice of Small Claim'. There will be a caption on the top of the first page in which they are clearly listed as a defendant. The body of the small claim will have a description of how the plaintiff feels they have been damaged by the defendant's actions. Depending on the state, the defendant may receive an actual form to write their response on, or they will be notified that they must file a response by a certain date to avoid a default judgment.

***IF YOU ARE A DEFENDANT IN A SMALL CLAIMS CASE, IT IS IMPERATIVE THAT YOU DO NOT IGNORE THE CLAIM!*** You must file a response. If you fail to do so, a default judgment will likely be entered against you and you will be forced to pay the plaintiff all of the damages they alleged in their claim, regardless of whether or not they are accurate.

Generally, a defendant can either pay the claim or return any property that was allegedly stolen, deny the claim and request a hearing, deny the claim and file a counter claim in small claims court, or request a jury trial. A sample of a completed response form is included in Appendix 1.

Regardless of their selection, the defendant does not need to allege any specific defenses at this point. They will have an opportunity to do so at the hearing. Depending on how a defendant responds, the case will proceed as follows:

- If they pay the claim: The defendant will need to send the plaintiff money and/or return the property in question directly to the plaintiff. They will also need to inform the court that they have paid the claim in full and submit proof of payment (such as a copy of a check made out to the plaintiff). They also may have to pay the filing and service fees that were incurred by the plaintiff (in addition to their own filing fee), depending on the state.
- If they request a hearing the case will proceed.
- If they file a counter claim, the plaintiff will then have to respond to the defendant's claim. However, this usually occurs at the actual hearing and the plaintiff does not have to file a written response (but check your local rules). The plaintiff just needs to be aware that they will need to offer a defense to the claims raised by the defendant.
- The case will then proceed to a hearing where both sides will have to prove their case and offer defenses to the opposing party's claims. There is usually space on a small claims response form where the defendant can allege their counterclaims (this happens most often in breach of contract claims, where both sides claim the other breached the contract and failed to perform in some way).

- If the defendant requests a jury trial, the plaintiff will then have a certain amount of time to refile their claim in the regular trial court. If they do not refile, their claim will be dismissed without prejudice (which means the plaintiff can refile), but they may have to reimburse the defendant for the filing fee they had to pay. If the plaintiff does file a formal complaint, the defendant will have to file an answer and the case will proceed in accordance with their state's normal trial court rules.
    - *If this option is available in the defendant's state, and they are certain that the plaintiff does not have the means or knowledge to prosecute their case in a regular trial (with or without a lawyer), requesting a jury trial can be an effective way to get a case dismissed as plaintiffs will often fail to file their circuit court complaint. That said, there is always the risk that the plaintiff will file the civil complaint, which means the defendant will now have to navigate the regular trial court system instead of defending themselves in small claims court.*

Regardless of how you choose to proceed, you *must* file your response within 14 days of being served with the notice of small claim. If you fail to respond, the plaintiff will likely seek a default judgment, which means the judge will award them all of the damages they requested.

## DEBT COLLECTION LAWSUITS

Many small claims cases are related to debt collection. Often, a third-party debt collector or the original lender will try and collect on past due credit cards, auto loans, and many other bills. While the basics of all debt collection lawsuits are the same as any other breach of contract case, defendants should keep in mind the following key points:

- Defendants in debt collection cases often have a hard time defending their case on the merits. For example, there is no dispute that they had a credit card and did not make the agreed upon payments. However, even when that is the case, filing a response and requesting a hearing are still worthwhile.
- Even if a defendant knows they are liable for the debt in question, they should still file a response denying the claims and request a hearing. Remember, the burden of proof is on the plaintiff! Make them provide evidence to support each element of their claim. Make them produce the actual agreement that was originally signed. If they are a third-party debt collector, make them produce the original agreement and the signed agreement wherein they purchased the debt. It is not uncommon for the plaintiff to be unable to produce these documents and their case will fail.
- Many debt collection cases are filed near the statute of limitations. The statute of limitations will begin to run from the time the defendant made the last payment on the debt. Defendant's should make the plaintiff produce evidence of the last payment they made. If they cannot do so, the defendant may have a good chance to get the case dismissed if there is no record of any payment made on the account within the statute of limitations period.
- Even if the plaintiff can produce all of the above documents, by requesting a hearing, the defendant

will show the plaintiff that they will not go down without a fight. This will go a long way toward settling the case. The plaintiff will be more likely to offer a fair settlement if they think they will have to expend additional time and resources gathering evidence and attending a small claims hearing.

- Finally, even if there is no defense on the merits, if the defendant can convince the plaintiff that they are judgment proof, they will likely be able to negotiate a good settlement. Being judgment proof means that the defendant has no garnishable assets for the plaintiff to collect. If the defendant is not working or is only working part time, they may not have enough wages for the plaintiff to garnish. If the defendant does not have much money in any bank accounts (or they only have retirement/social security funds that are protected from garnishment) and they have no other garnishable property, the plaintiff will likely accept a very low settlement offer.
- In the alternative, some defendants may want to let the plaintiff get their judgment if they are confident the plaintiff will not be able to take any kind of garnishment action against them. Keep in mind that judgments are usually valid for 10-20 years. However, there is nothing to stop a defendant from negotiating a settlement after a judgment is entered. If the plaintiff is convinced that they will not be able to collect, they may be willing to settle for a small amount. For example, a defendant can inform the plaintiff they are judgment proof (they should not be afraid to provide evidence supporting this assertion if the plaintiff asks for it), but they are able to borrow a

certain amount of money from friends or family to make a onetime payment to settle the case.

When negotiating a settlement, a good rule of thumb for defendants is not to accept anything less than a 50% discount on the alleged damages (or the outstanding judgment). However, the standards for settlement varies quite a bit among debt collectors. Some may readily accept a deal for 50% or less of the outstanding balance. If the defendant is actually judgment proof (or close to it), they may be able to negotiate an even better deal.

Now that a small claim has been filed and responded to, the next step is for both sides to find and prepare evidence before the hearing.

# CHAPTER 5: HOW TO FIND, PREPARE, AND INTRODUCE

# EVIDENCE

A plaintiff (or a defendant alleging counterclaims) proves their claims by submitting evidence that shows each element of their claim is present. Likewise, a defendant will usually attempt to show that the plaintiff has not proven all the elements of their claim by also submitting evidence (or by simply informing the court that the plaintiff has failed to address an element of their claim). The vast majority of evidence consists of witness testimony and written documentation. Although your state will have an evidence code that governs what is and is not considered admissible evidence in a regular trial, these rules are often quite a bit more relaxed in small claims court and a judge is usually not required to follow them precisely. Nevertheless, they will still be using the rules of evidence as a guide and may refuse to allow you to submit documentation or testimony if it does not comply with your state's code. Whether you are a plaintiff or defendant, follow the steps below to procure your evidence and prepare it for the small claims hearing.

## PROCURING WITNESSES

Put simply, a witness is anyone who testifies under oath in a court proceeding. Generally speaking, a witness should have firsthand knowledge of the events they are testifying about (if they do not have firsthand knowledge, the opposing side will likely object to their testimony as hearsay – see Chapter 6). Below are three examples (referenced in Chapter 2) of situations that could (and often do) end up in small claims court. Below the examples are a list of who could potentially be valuable witnesses:

**Example 1:**

Plaintiff claims they were shopping in a supermarket when they slipped and fell in a puddle of water, injuring their back. This caused Plaintiff $1,500 in medical bills and they will seek an additional $1,500 for pain, suffering, and inconvenience. In this type of negligence case, Plaintiff would allege that Defendant (the store owner) has a duty to keep their store safe for customers and by failing to keep the floors dry and clean, Defendant failed in that duty, causing Plaintiff damages.

**Example 2:**

Plaintiff claims that the defendant owed them $5,000 because they had entered into an oral agreement in which Plaintiff agreed to paint the outside of Defendant's house in exchange for $7,000. Defendant paid Plaintiff $2000 up front, but then failed to pay the additional $5000 after Plaintiff finished painting the house.

**Example 3:**

Plaintiff claims that Defendant (who is Plaintiff's former roommate) stole his flat screen television and antique motorcycle when Defendant moved out. Plaintiff seeks damages of $6,000, representing $1,000 for the value of the television, $3,000 for the value of the motorcycle, and $2,000 in non-economic damages for loss of use of the property and/or pain/suffering/inconvenience. In the alternative, Plaintiff seeks return of the property in good condition and $2,000 in non-economic damages for loss of use of the property and/or pain/suffering/inconvenience.

Using the above examples, potential witnesses for each scenario would be:

**Potential Witnesses from Example 1:**

Other shoppers who saw Plaintiff fall or saw the puddle on the floor would be ideal here. Of course, unless they are companions of Plaintiff, he or she may not know their names or how to contact them. In addition, any employee of the grocery store that may have seen the puddle or had a duty to clean it up could provide valuable testimony (see below for information on how to compel such witnesses to testify at the hearing).

**Potential Witnesses from Example 2:**

In this example, Plaintiff would want anyone who knew of the existence of the agreement to testify. Did someone help Plaintiff paint the house? Was this person aware of the terms of the agreement? If Plaintiff painted other houses, can someone testify as to what Plaintiff normally charged for similar jobs? Did Plaintiff complain to others about not getting paid the full amount around the time Defendant refused to pay?

**Potential Witnesses from Example 3:**

Did Plaintiff have another roommate besides Defendant? Was someone with Plaintiff when he bought the TV or motorcycle? Has anyone seen Defendant in possession of the motorcycle and/or TV?

Can anyone testify that Plaintiff used to own these items and how much he valued them?

Regardless of who ends up being a witness in your case, make sure that any witness you have testify is only testifying regarding a crucial element or defense of your claim and try to avoid having multiple witnesses that will testify about the exact same thing.

If the witness is a friend or relative and you can trust them to show up at trial, then you should not have any trouble making sure they are available to testify. However, what if you need an unfriendly witness to offer testimony? In that case, you will need to have the court issue a subpoena on your behalf that orders them to appear at the time and date of the small claims hearing.

**How to Subpoena a Witness:**

As officers of the court, attorneys are allowed to subpoena witnesses and compel them to appear in court. As a party to a small claims case representing yourself, you do not have such power. Instead, you will need to fill out a subpoena on your own and then have the court issue the subpoena for you. You will still be the one in charge of making sure the witness is actually served with a copy of the subpoena. Most courthouses will have blank subpoena forms that you can fill out with the details of your particular case. Samples of filled out subpoena forms from the state of Oregon are included in Appendix 1.

Once the subpoena form is complete, you will need to go back to the courthouse and present it to the clerk at the civil filing window. The clerk will make sure everything is in order and then sign it and stamp it with the court's seal (this process may vary by state). This gives the subpoena duces tecum the official authority of the court and anyone who disregards it can potentially be found in contempt.

Next, you will need to serve the subpoena on the witness. In some states, subpoenas can be served by the party in the case, which means you do not have to pay for the sheriff or a private process server to deliver the subpoena. That said, it is often more convenient to pay a professional process server or the sheriff to deliver the subpoena and that is the recommended course of action if you can afford the expense.

In any case, subpoenas for witnesses usually need to be served personally. In addition, most states require that witnesses be compensated for their time and reimbursed for travel costs (usually in the form of a per mile rate). Check your local rules of civil procedure and trial court rules to find out your state's witness and mileage fees.

When you issue a subpoena, you should include a check for the appropriate amount. To determine the proper mileage, use any mapping web application (google maps, etc.) to determine the proper roundtrip distance from the witness's address. Then, multiply that amount by the mileage rate and add it to the witness fee. It is helpful to write up a simple calculation and attach it to the subpoena, but it is not necessary.

Once the witness has been properly served with a court-issued subpoena and given the proper compensation, they are legally obligated to appear and answer your questions under oath. If the date arrives and the witness has not shown up, you will have good cause to request a new date for the hearing (alternatively, if you feel the witness' testimony is not crucial and you are eager to have your day in court, you can still proceed without them). Simply inform the judge that a key witness has failed to appear pursuant to a validly issued subpoena (make sure you have a copy available to review) and the interests of justice require that a new hearing date be set so the witness can be heard.

# PROCURING EXHIBITS:

In addition to having witnesses testify on your behalf, you will usually want to submit written (or audio/video) evidence that also supports your claim and reinforces the testimony of your witnesses. An exhibit can essentially be anything, but 99% of the time, it will be some sort of document. As witnesses are often biased and have imperfect memories, cold, hard documentary evidence can be vital to proving a claim or defense.

**How to Identify Potential Exhibits:**

As with witnesses, a relevant exhibit is anything that helps prove or disprove a party's claim or defense. Exhibits that are repetitive are usually unnecessary. Similarly, exhibits should be as concise as possible (don't submit five years of timesheets when wages are disputed for only two specific years). Using the examples from earlier in the chapter, here are some types of written evidence that would be useful to both parties:

**Example 1:**

- Medical bills that show any out of pocket medical expenses.
- Any kind of accident report that was filled out by the grocery store.
- Any cleaning logs that are maintained by the grocery store.
- Any emails, text messages, or other documents wherein Plaintiff describes his/her injuries and the pain, suffering, and/or inconvenience they have caused.

**Example 2:**

- Any invoices or receipts sent to Defendant by Plaintiff.
- Any similar invoices or receipts from prior similar jobs performed by Plaintiff for other people.
- Any emails, text messages, or other documents wherein Plaintiff describes the work done for Defendant and how much Plaintiff was supposed to get paid.

**Example 3:**

- Any receipt that shows what Plaintiff paid for the TV or motorcycle.
- A website or advertisement that shows the value of the same model of TV and motorcycle that were allegedly stolen by Defendant.
- Any receipts for maintenance showing that Plaintiff paid for the upkeep of the TV and motorcycle.
- Any emails or text messages that Plaintiff sent to Defendant wherein the TV or motorcycle were discussed.

Once you are aware of what types of exhibits would be helpful in proving your claim or defense, you will need to obtain them. As with witnesses, exhibits can be obtained by having the court issue a subpoena. A subpoena for documents is usually referred to as a 'Subpoena Duces Tecum' (Latin for 'you shall bring with you')[4]. It is issued by the court the same way as a subpoena for a witness is issued. However, a subpoena duces tecum generally does not need

---

[4] Although a person does not normally bring the documents 'with them'. Rather, they are commanded to deliver the documents to a specific location (usually via mail to the party's address). The person's actual appearance is not required.

to be served personally. It can usually be served via mail (certified mail is recommended, so you will have proof that the subpoena was sent).

If you think you need a police report to help prove your claims, you can usually obtain these without a subpoena. You will need to contact the relevant police department and inquire about their particular procedures for releasing police reports. Make sure you do so well in advance of your trial, as the process can take several weeks.

Once the subpoena form is complete, you will need to go to the courthouse and present it to the clerk at the civil filing window. As with a regular subpoena, the clerk will make sure everything is in order and then sign it and stamp it with the court's seal (as with other subpoenas, this process may vary by state). Before you mail the subpoena duces tecum to a third party, you usually need to send a copy to the opposing party (to put them on notice of the documents you are seeking) and then wait a certain number of days. After that you can send the subpoena duces tecum to the addressee. You will also have to send any applicable witness fee along with the subpoena, but you do not need to include any mileage payment.

Once the person or entity has been properly served with a court-issued subpoena duces tecum and received the required witness fee, they are legally obligated to turn over the documents requested or face potential contempt charges. If the time to produce the documents has passed without a response, you should contact the person directly and inform them that you will be pursuing contempt charges if they do not respond.[5] If the hearing date is approaching and you still do not have the documents that were requested pursuant to a valid subpoena, you can ask the court to delay the

---

[5] If the person who was served believes they have good legal cause to disregard the subpoena, they should file a motion to quash the subpoena; not simply ignore it.

proceedings and/or seek contempt charges against the person/entity failing to produce the documents.

A sample of a subpoena duces tecum from the State of Oregon is included in Appendix 1.

**Preparing Exhibits:**

On the day of your hearing, you will need to bring four copies of all your exhibits. One copy is for you, one for the opposing party, one for witnesses to review, and one for the judge. All exhibits must be numbered in the bottom right of the document, with plaintiffs usually starting with the number 1 (Exhibit 1, Exhibit 2, etc.) and defendants usually starting with number 101 (Exhibit 101, Exhibit 102, etc.).

In addition to the exhibits being marked, they must also have individual page numbers (with each individual exhibit starting over with 'page 1'). The easiest way to label exhibits is to have them scanned as a PDF file and then use an editing tool to add the label. We recommend using PDFill, which is free and can be downloaded here: http://www.pdfill.com. If you are unable to use a PDF file editor and/or you only have a few short exhibits, you can simply label each one by hand. If you are submitting photographs as exhibits, you should group them by subject and label each group as a different exhibit, with each individual photo having its own page number.

If you wish, you may put each set of exhibits in a binder, but the judge will likely not care how they are bound if you only have a few exhibits, so long as they are clearly labeled and each page can be referenced and viewed easily. You should also include a witness and exhibit list at the front of each set of exhibits. Simply list your exhibits in roughly the order you intend to introduce them and give a brief description of each one. Do the same for your witnesses, but do not be concerned if you end up calling witnesses or introducing exhibits out of order.

Now that your exhibits and witnesses are prepared, you are almost ready to go to court! Read on to learn what to expect at the hearing!

# CHAPTER 6: AT THE SMALL CLAIMS HEARING

This chapter goes over the typical steps involved in any small claims hearing. Do not be intimidated by the fact that you will be in a courtroom in front of a judge. With this guide you will be well prepared to put on your case.

## MEDIATION

Many jurisdictions require parties to attend a mediation session before the small claims hearing. Even if mediation is not required, your jurisdiction may very well have an optional mediation program. This may be the same day as the hearing, but it may also be scheduled a week or two beforehand. If mediation is required, both parties will need to meet with a neutral mediator. This mediator will likely be a court employee who will try to work out a solution that is agreeable to both parties. If a solution is reached, the agreement will be entered on the record and both sides can be brought back into court if they fail to honor the agreement. If a solution is not reached, the case will proceed to the hearing.

On the day of your hearing you should be prepared to present your case before the judge. You are essentially acting as your own attorney and, although the rules may be somewhat relaxed in small claims court, you should conduct yourself as an attorney would to the extent possible. Here are some general guidelines:

- Get to court early. Parking may be inconvenient, you will likely have to go through security, and it may take time to find out which courtroom you are in. Make sure you give yourself time for all of these issues.
- Be respectful to the judge and the opposing party.
- Dress professionally. It is always surprising how many people show up to court in casual clothes. Although there is no dress code required for parties or witnesses, taking the time to dress professionally shows the judge that you are taking everything seriously and lends an air of respectability to your claims.
- DO NOT argue with each other in front of the judge. Both sides will have a chance to present their arguments, examine witnesses, and make a closing statement. There is no need to interrupt the other person when it is their turn to talk.
- Do not talk over the judge, the opposing party, or any witnesses.
- If you do not understand something the judge has said or how to proceed, simply ASK! A judge will not give you legal advice, but they will inform you if you need help with procedural questions (of course, if you read this guide, such questions should be rare).

- When addressing the judge, it is always proper to stand up first. It is not necessary to stand when examining witnesses, but you may do so if you prefer. DO NOT roam around the courtroom like you may have seen on TV!

## STEPS AT THE HEARING

The small claims hearing will generally proceed as follows:

1. The judge will call your case by name and case number. When they do, you may approach the counsel table from the gallery.
2. Once the judge is sure everyone is ready and there are no procedural issues to deal with, they may ask both parties (starting with the plaintiff) to make an opening statement. If you want to make an opening statement, but the judge seems to skip over this step, you can always ask to make one. Just keep it brief and summarize why you are entitled to relief.
3. At this point, the judge may want both parties to submit all their exhibits and offer any relevant objections. If you feel you have good cause to object to any evidence being entered into the record inform the judge of the specific exhibit you are objecting to and why (see below for the most common objections you will deal with in small claims court). Do not be afraid to object! The worst that will happen is that the judge will overrule your objection and the evidence will be received (which is what will definitely happen if you do not object).
4. The judge will then tell the plaintiff to call their first witness. Say, "Thank you, Your Honor. I call XXXX." At this point, the

plaintiff's witness should proceed to the witness stand and they will be sworn in by the court clerk or the judge. Once sworn in, ask your questions (see below for tips on examining witnesses). During questioning, the judge may interject with their own questions.

5. If the judge did not admit some or all of your exhibits at the beginning of the trial, you will need to make sure that your exhibits are admitted at the time they come up during witness testimony (regardless of which party has called the witness). For example, if you are interviewing a witness and ask them to review Exhibit 2, have the witness describe the exhibit, then say, "Your honor, I would like to admit Exhibit 2 into the record." The judge will give the opposing party an opportunity to object and then make a decision on whether or not the exhibit is received. The fact that you have already handed your exhibits to the witness and the judge does not mean they are admitted, unless the judge has already clearly stated as much before the hearing!

6. After the plaintiff has finished asking their witness questions, the defendant will have an opportunity to cross-examine the witness and ask them any questions that are relevant to any claim or defense. When the defendant is done with their cross examination, the plaintiff will have a chance to ask any follow up questions (called 'redirect examination'), but they will likely be restricted to only asking about issues that were brought up in the defendant's cross-examination (although the judge will probably grant a party some leniency in this regard in small claims court). After both parties have asked all their questions, the plaintiff will call their next witness.

7. Once the plaintiff has called all of their witnesses and introduced all of their exhibits, they will inform the judge that they rest their case. If they still have exhibits that were not

admitted during examination and they still want the judge to consider them, they should state that they have additional exhibits they would like to enter into the record before they rest.
8. At this point, the defendant will have the chance to call witnesses and introduce exhibits. The plaintiff will have the chance to cross examine each witness and object as appropriate.
9. After the defendant has called all of their witnesses and rested their case, the plaintiff will then have the chance to call rebuttal witnesses who can contradict the statements made by the defendant's witnesses. These can be new witnesses or witnesses who initially testified during the presentation of the plaintiff's case, but the testimony will be restricted only to rebutting information that was presented by the defendant.
10. Once rebuttal testimony is complete, the judge will ask for a closing statement from both parties. If you are the plaintiff, you should inform the judge how you have proven each element of your claim, citing the specific testimony or exhibit that illustrates your point. If you are the defendant, inform the judge how the plaintiff has failed to prove the elements of their claims.
11. The judge will likely make a ruling on the spot, but may issue a written opinion in a few days if they feel they need time to review the evidence.
12. If the judge/jury rules in your favor, CONGRATULATIONS! You have successfully prosecuted/defended a small claims case from start to finish! Continue to Chapter 7 for information on how to collect on your judgment.
13. If you are the plaintiff and the judge rules in the defendant's favor, you will likely have to pay their filing fee and any other court costs incurred by the defendant. If the defendant filed

a counterclaim against you, you will be ordered to pay on that claim as well (unless the judge decided that neither party had proven their respective claims). The judge will prepare a judgment stating as much and your case will be over. It may be small consolation, but if you followed the steps in this guide, you can at least rest assured that you gave it your best shot and did everything you could to obtain relief.
14. Many states do not allow any appeals of small claims judgments, while some allow appeals in certain circumstances. Regardless, how to appeal a small claims decision is beyond the scope of this guide. Just be aware that if you think you have good cause to appeal, you will need to do so within the time limit set by your state (such as 30 days after the judgment is entered, for example).

# EXAMINING WITNESSES

On the day of the hearing, after any opening statements have been made, the judge will ask the plaintiff to call their first witness (and, of course, the defendant will call their witnesses after the plaintiff rests their case). The plaintiff will do so and begin asking questions relevant to their claims. The first step is to establish why the witness is testifying. Who are they? How do they know the plaintiff/defendant? What knowledge do they have that proves an element of a claim or defense? As always, keep things simple and direct. Apply who, what, where, why, questions. Do not argue with the witness (but do not be afraid to ask for clarification if you feel their answer doesn't make sense).

After the plaintiff has asked their first witness all their questions, the defendant will have the chance to cross-examine the witness. In small claims court, parties are usually allowed to directly examine witnesses on cross-examination, which means the party cross-examining the witness will be able to ask the witness any questions that are relevant to any claim or defense. This eliminates the need to recall witnesses, avoids needless repetition, and makes things move along faster. After cross-examination, the other party will have a chance to follow up with any questions on redirect examination. After that, the witness will be excused and the plaintiff will call their next witness.

Of course, in addition to examining witnesses, plaintiffs and defendants will most likely want to testify themselves, as well. With no attorney to ask you questions, you will simply offer your testimony directly to the court. Explain that you would like to call yourself as a witness (you will most likely be able to testify from the counsel table; rather than having to go up to the witness stand). After you are sworn it, you will then be able to offer your version of events in a clear and concise manner. If you want to review an exhibit, inform the court and the opposing party, tell the court why that particular exhibit is significant, and ask to enter it into the record (if it has not already been entered). Just remember that you are testifying; that is, you are stating facts on the record. Now is not the time to argue the merits of your case. Save all your opinions for your closing statement and simply stick to the facts.

## OBJECTIONS

Remember, a judge in small claims court is usually not bound by their state's evidence code, but they will be using it as a guide when deciding what is and is not admissible. For the purposes of a small claims hearing, there are really only two types of evidentiary objections you need to be aware of: Relevance and Hearsay. These are by far the most common objections in any civil proceeding. Understanding them will make you well prepared for your small claims hearing.

**Relevance:**

A typical evidentiary rule regarding the relevance of an exhibit will look something like this: 'All relevant evidence is admissible, except as otherwise provided by the Evidence Code, by the Constitutions of the United States and [this state], or by statutory and decisional law. Evidence which is not relevant is not admissible.'

Additionally, a typical definition of 'relevant evidence' would be: "Evidence having any tendency to make the existence of any fact that is of consequence to the determination of the action more probable or less probable than it would be without the evidence."

Pretty straightforward, right? If evidence is relevant to any claim or defense, it is admissible. If it is not relevant, then it is not admissible and an objection should be made. Often, relevance objections come up when one party tries to make the other side look bad by introducing some fact that has nothing to do with the elements of the party's claim. Examples of irrelevant evidence include:
- In a battery case, evidence that the defendant was arrested for driving under the influence of intoxicants one month before the alleged battery took place.
- In a breach of contract case, evidence that the defendant breached a contract with a third party a year earlier would likely not be relevant to the present case (as prior bad acts are no indication that a party acted the same way in the present case as they did in the prior case).

- In a personal injury case involving damages for a broken arm, evidence that the plaintiff broke their leg a few years ago would not be relevant.

Although there are more detailed rules of evidence that may apply in some situations, think of the relevance objection as a catch-all objection and do not spend time trying to remember whether or not a more specific objection exists. So long as you can make the case that the evidence in question is not relevant to any claim or defense, offering an objection based on relevance is perfectly acceptable. If you are unsure of whether or not evidence is relevant, always err on the side of caution and object. The worst thing that will happen is that your objection will be overruled and the evidence will be entered into the record (which would happen anyway if you did not object).

**Hearsay:**

Typically, 'Hearsay' is defined as: 'A statement, other than one made by the declarant while testifying at the trial or hearing, offered in evidence to prove the truth of the matter asserted.' A 'statement' can be oral, written, or any type of nonverbal contact. The 'declarant' is simply the person who originally made the statement in the first place. In other words, a witness cannot testify that someone else told them something.[6] The person who actually made the statement needs to be present to testify. Examples of hearsay evidence include:
- In a custody hearing if the husband were to testify: "my wife's sister told me that my wife abuses the children when I am not around."

---

[6] Likewise, a document written by someone else cannot be admitted as an exhibit (unless an exception applies).

- In a breach of contract case, if the plaintiff were to testify: "Defendant's former employee told me that Defendant had no intention of honoring our agreement."
- In a personal injury case, if the plaintiff tried to submit a copy of a text message from a bystander that said they saw the defendant run a red light and hit the plaintiff's car.

Although hearsay evidence is generally inadmissible, there are several exceptions. The most common hearsay exceptions relate to statements made by the party opponent (meaning a witness for the plaintiff can testify that the defendant told them something and vice versa) and business records, such as time sheets and paystubs.

Regardless of the legal exceptions to the standard hearsay rule, in small claims court a judge will most likely allow hearsay evidence if they feel it is sufficiently reliable and you should not trouble yourself with trying to learn all of the hearsay exceptions. That said, you should still object to evidence that is clearly hearsay (especially if it is similar to the blatant examples mentioned above). When hearsay evidence is admitted (regardless of whether or not you offered an objection), in your closing statement you should definitely make a point of reminding the judge that the evidence should be given very little weight and the court should not consider it credible when making a decision.[7]

With a basic understanding of relevance and hearsay, you will be well equipped to prosecute or defend your case in small claims court and examine witnesses effectively. Just remember to keep things focused on the elements of your specific claim or defense.

---

[7] Of course, if you are the one trying to admit hearsay evidence, you should argue the opposite: even if the evidence is hearsay, the person making the statement in court is sufficiently credible and the judge should trust this person's sworn testimony when evaluating the merits of the case.

Regardless of how a hearing was resolved, one party will almost certainly have received some type of monetary award, even if it is just the filing fee that the winning side was forced to pay to appear in the case. The next chapter discusses how to collect on a judgment that includes a monetary award.

# CHAPTER 7: HOW TO COLLECT ON A JUDGMENT

If you have prevailed in small claims court, congratulations! You should be proud that you prosecuted or defended your case without an attorney! Unfortunately, winning in court is often only half the battle as many parties ordered to pay will refuse to do so. When this happens, the burden is on the person who is owed money to collect what is due.

If you have prevailed against a government agency or a large corporation, getting paid will likely not be a problem. But if you have a valid judgment against an individual, you may be required to undertake collection efforts. For small claims litigants representing themselves, the two best courses of action are usually garnishing bank accounts and garnishing wages.[8]

**Relevant Definitions:**

---

[8] Even though attorneys are not allowed to represent people in small claims court, they can help prevailing parties collect on a judgment. The fact that you have a valid judgment may entice many attorneys to undertake collection efforts on a contingency basis if you do not want to attempt collecting on your judgment by yourself.

When trying to collect on a judgment, you should be familiar with the following terms (remember, the exact terms may vary by state).

**Judgment Creditor:** A person who is owed money from a judgment debtor due to a court judgment (the prevailing party in a civil action).

**Judgment Debtor:** A person who owes money to a judgment creditor due to a court judgment.

**Writ of Garnishment:** A writ of garnishment is a court order that requires a third party (such as a bank or employer) to turn over property it holds or has control over that belongs to the judgment debtor (such as bank account funds or wages).

**Garnishee:** A third party who has been ordered to hand over any property of a judgment debtor it has in its custody or control.

**Garnishor:** The person or entity who is issuing the garnishment. As officers of the court, attorneys are allowed to issue garnishments directly on behalf of their clients. If you are acting *pro se*, you will likely need the court issue the garnishment on your behalf, but you will still be considered the garnishor.

## GARNISHING BANK ACCOUNTS

If you (the judgment creditor) happen to know where the judgment debtor has any bank accounts, you can seek to have those garnished. With few exceptions, if a bank has been served with a valid garnishment, they are required to turn over any and all funds of the judgment debtor over to you (up to the amount owed under the judgment). Although there is quite a bit of paperwork involved, the general process of garnishing a bank account is relatively simple.

Of course, be sure to check your state's laws regarding garnishment procedure.

Garnishing a bank account generally requires that you fill out a writ of garnishment, have it issued by the court (similar to how they issue subpoenas), and then send that writ to the bank along with instructions. Note that you may also be required to send other forms, such as a garnishee response form. You will also likely be required to send a copy of the writ and some type of objection form to the judgment debtor to put them on notice that their bank account has been garnished.

Using Oregon as an example, a judgment creditor would need to send the following documents to the garnishee and the judgment debtor:

**NOTE: The section below should be viewed as an example only!!! If you do not live in Oregon your state's garnishment procedure will likely vary considerably! You must check your state's garnishment laws!*

**Documents to be Sent to the Garnishee (ORS 18.650):**

- **Writ of Garnishment:** As mentioned above, this is the official order that requires the garnishee to turn over the property.
- **Garnishee Response Form:** This is the form that the garnishee must fill out and return to you, even if they do not hold any property of the judgment debtor. Per Oregon law, they must return the form to you within seven business days.
- **Garnishee Instructions:** These are standard instructions issued to the garnishee.
- **Wage Exemption Calculation Form:** This is the form used by the garnishee to calculate how much of a debtor's wages

should be garnished (see the 'GARNISHING WAGES' section below for more information).
- **Search Fee:** In Oregon, if you are sending a writ of garnishment to a bank or other financial institution, you are required to pay them $15 for the trouble of searching their records. A search fee is not required when garnishing a debtor's wages.

**Documents to be Sent to the Judgment Debtor (ORS 18.658):**

- **Writ of Garnishment:** Described above.
- **Debt Calculation Form:** This is the form used to show the debtor exactly how you arrived at the appropriate garnishment amount. You will have to deduct any payments that have been made on the outstanding judgment.
- **Notice of Exemptions:** This is a list of standard garnishment exemptions that you need to send to the debtor so they know if they have good cause to challenge the garnishment. Examples of exemptions include funds paid as child support, Social Security income, and other government financial assistance
- **Challenge to Garnishment Form:** This is the form a debtor can use to challenge the garnishment. However, they can only challenge the garnishment if they have good cause to believe the funds in question fall within one of the exemptions. They cannot use this form to challenge the underlying validity of the judgment or the amount awarded.

Although the exact type and name of the forms will vary, your state's garnishment procedure will be similar. Once your particular state's garnishment forms are ready, you will need to take them to the courthouse and present them to the court clerk. You will likely need to pay the court a fee for issuing the writ. The clerk will make sure the writ is complete and then they will ascribe the court's seal to it. Note that some courts may take a few days to approve the writ, in which case they will notify you when it is ready to pick up. Attaching the court's seal makes the writ official and it will have the full authority of the court behind it. Make sure you make at least two copies (and probably a third for your records).

You will then need to mail all of the appropriate forms to the garnishee and the judgment debtor in the manner prescribed by state law.

Unless your state specifically requires you to do so, DO NOT mail the forms to the judgment debtor at the same time that you mail them to the garnishee. If you do, you run the risk of the judgment debtor emptying their bank account before the bank has the chance to seize the funds. Instead, you should wait 7-10 days and then mail them to the judgment debtor. This will give the bank enough time to review your writ and determine if they have any funds subject to garnishment. Most states also require that you hold any funds obtained for a certain number of days before you spend it, in order to give the debtor time to file a challenge to the garnishment.

## GARNISHING WAGES

Garnishing wages works in much the same way as garnishing bank accounts. You will need to fill out all the required forms and send them to the employer and the judgment debtor. Generally, a certain percentage of a judgment debtor's disposable wages will be immune from garnishment. Furthermore, any garnishment that would reduce the judgment debtor's disposable income below a minimum threshold will not be allowed. This means that very low wage earners and/or part time employees may not have sufficient income to be subject to garnishment (although many minimum wage, full time employees will still likely have some funds that are available).

Although there is a lot of paperwork involved, garnishing wages and bank accounts is not difficult. In most cases, the hardest part is finding out whether the judgment creditor has a job and/or where they hold their bank accounts. Do not be discouraged if you are not able to initially collect on your judgment. Money judgments are valid for several years and can often be renewed for an additional amount of time. What's more, money awards usually earn interest at rates much better than most stable investments. Just because the judgment debtor does not have any assets or income now, does not mean they won't be in a better position in a few years. If you sit tight, you will likely be able to collect on your judgment in the future and earn a respectable amount of interest.

# CONCLUSION

If you have read this guide you will have a firm understanding of how small claims proceed in state court. Although we cannot guarantee success, reading this guide will definitely give you an advantage over any opposing party that has not bothered taking similar steps.

Showing the judge you are well prepared and understand how the civil legal system works will give your arguments an air of credibility, especially if your case comes down to believing the testimony of one party over the other. A plaintiff or defendant who shows up unprepared always comes off as less trustworthy, even when their actual claims may have some merit.

Win or lose, you can rest assured that by purchasing this guide and following its advice, you put on a good case. You can hold your head high, knowing that you put on a strong effort based on sound legal theories and a competent understanding of the small claims process. Thank you for your purchase and good luck!

***If you enjoyed this book, please leave a positive review on amazon.com!***

# APPENDIX 1: SAMPLE PLEADINGS

These samples are based on actual pleadings used by the author in the State of Oregon (where he practices law). They are included here to illustrate how such pleadings might look, but the formatting rules of your particular state will vary! We cannot guarantee that using this format to draft your documents will be accepted in other states! Please check your court's statutes and court rules!

IN THE CIRCUIT COURT FOR THE STATE OF OREGON

FOR THE COUNTY OF CLACKAMAS
Small Claims Department

| | |
|---|---|
| JOHN SMITH, <br><br> Plaintiff, <br><br> v. <br><br> MARK JONES, <br><br> Defendant. | Case No.: 18SC12345 <br><br> SMALL CLAIM AND NOTICE OF SMALL CLAIM |

**PLAINTIFF:**
John Smith
123 Fake St.
Oregon City, OR 97045
503-123-4567

**DEFENDANT:**
Mark Jones
987 Phony Ave.
Canby, OR 97013
503-987-6543

I, Plaintiff, claim that on or about 12/09/2017, the above-named Defendant owed me: the sum of $1,500 because: I entered into an oral contract with Defendant to paint the outside of his house in exchange for $2,000. Defendant paid me $500 up front, but failed to pay the additional amount when I completed the job on 12/09/2017. Defendant has received the benefit of having a painted house, but has refused to pay the agreed upon price. Defendant's actions have damaged me in the amount of $1,500, and this amount is still due.

I have paid (or will pay):

Filing Fee:   $55

Service Costs: $45

| | |
|---|---|
| Claim: | $1,500 |
| + Fees: | $55 |
| + Costs: | $45 |
| **TOTAL:** | **$1,600** |

SMALL CLAIM AND NOTICE OF SMALL CLAIM
Page 1 of 3

## DECLARATION OF GOOD FAITH EFFORT

I, Plaintiff, have made a good faith effort to collect this claim from Defendant before filing this claim with the court clerk. The efforts I took are as follows: On 12/10/2017, I spoke with Defendant on the telephone and told him to pay what he owed me. He told me he would pay, but I did not hear from him again. I again spoke to him on the phone on 12/30/2017 and demanded payment. This time he refused to pay.

**I hereby declare that the above statements are true to the best of my knowledge and belief. I understand they are made for use in court and I am subject to penalty for perjury.**

Dated: 1/16/2018

_____
Plaintiff's Signature

JOHN SMITH

**DEFENDANT'S REGISTERED AGENT: N/A**
(only if Defendant is a business)

# NOTICE TO DEFENDANT:
## READ THESE PAPERS CAREFULLY!

Within **14 DAYS\*** after receiving this notice you MUST do ONE of the following things in writing:

- Pay the claim plus filing fees and service expenses paid by plaintiff (send payment directly to the plaintiff, not to the court) **OR**,
- Demand a hearing and pay the fee required (below) **OR**,
- Demand a jury trial and pay the fee required (below). This option is available only if amount claimed is more than $750.

If you fail to do one of the above within **14 DAYS\*** after you get this notice, the plaintiff may ask the court to enter a judgment against you. The judgment will be for the amount of the claim, plus filing fees and service costs paid by the plaintiff, plus a prevailing party fee. If you are not able to respond in time because you are in active military service of the United States, talk to a legal advisor about the Servicemembers Civil Relief Act.

**COURT NAME / ADDRESS / PHONE #**
Clackamas County Circuit Court
807 Main St.
Oregon City, OR 97045      503-655-8447

**Defendant's Filing Fees** (must be filled in by the PLAINTIFF):

(1) To demand a hearing if the amount claimed is $2,500 or less: **$55**.

(2) To demand a hearing if the amount claimed is more than $2,500: **$99**.

(3) To demand a jury trial (only if amount claimed is over $750: **$165**.

If you have questions about filing procedures, go to www.courts.oregon.gov. Or you may contact the court clerk. The clerk cannot give you legal advice about the claim.

**\*NOTE:** If the plaintiff is an inmate (ORS 30.642) AND the defendant is a government agency or other public body (ORS 30.260), the defendant must respond within 30 days after receiving this Notice.

**SMALL CLAIM AND NOTICE OF SMALL CLAIM**

**IN THE CIRCUIT COURT FOR THE STATE OF OREGON**
**FOR THE COUNTY OF CLACKAMAS**
**Small Claims Department**

JOHN SMITH,

        Plaintiff,

v.

MARK JONES,

        Defendant.

Case No.: 18SC12345

**DEFENDANT'S RESPONSE**

☐ PAYMENT OF CLAIM:
Proof of payment (including fees and costs) to Plaintiff is attached (or proof that the requested property was returned to Plaintiff).

Total Amount Paid: N/A (or) Describe property and method of return: N/A.

☒ DENIAL OF CLAIM:
I deny Plaintiff's claim and demand a ☒ hearing [**or**] : ☐ jury trial (*claim must be for more than $750 (without fees and costs) to request a jury trial*).

☐ COUNTERCLAIM:
*Counterclaims must arise out of the same transaction or event as Plaintiff's claim.*
I make the following counterclaim against Plaintiff for $ N/A.

I, Defendant, claim that on or about [*date*], the above-named Plaintiff owed me the amount claimed because: N/A.

If the amount is the value of property that you believe should be given to you, describe the

property: N/A.

Dated: 1/25/2018

                                                      _____
                                                      Mark Jones
                                                      987 Phony Ave.
                                                      Canby, OR 97013
                                                      503-987-6543

**DEFENDANT'S RESPONSE**
Page 1 of 1

IN THE CIRCUIT COURT FOR THE STATE OF OREGON
FOR THE COUNTY OF CLACKAMAS
Small Claims Department

| | |
|---|---|
| JOHN SMITH,<br><br>        Plaintiff,<br><br>v.<br><br>MARK JONES,<br><br>        Defendant. | Case No.: 18SC12345<br><br>CERTIFICATE OF SERVICE |

I, Jane Williams, declare that I am a resident of the state of Oregon. I am a competent person 18 years of age or older and not a party to or a lawyer in this case. I certify that I served the following documents on the person named below on 1/03/2018:

**SMALL CLAIM AND NOTICE OF SMALL CLAIM**
**DEFENDANT'S RESPONSE**

Defendant Mark Jones was served at 987 Phony Ave., Canby, OR 97013 by the following method:

| | |
|---|---|
| ☒ By hand delivery<br>☐ By first class mail<br>☐ By certified mail, RRR, restricted delivery<br>(copy of return receipt attached) | ☐ By substitute service, per ORCP 7D(2)(b)<br>☐ By office service, per ORCP 7D(2)(c)<br><br>☐ Other: _____ |

**Certificate of Document Preparation.**
I certify that (check all boxes and complete all blanks that apply):
    A. ☒ I completed this document myself, but I used a template and instructions purchased from a commercial business without receiving any personal legal advice.
    B. ☐ I paid or will pay _____ for help in completing and/or reviewing this document.

I hereby declare that the above statements are true to the best of my knowledge and belief. I understand they are made for use in court and I am subject to penalty for perjury.

Dated: 1/10/2018                              _____
                                                      Signature
                                                      Jane Williams
                                                      55 Main St., Oregon City, OR 97045
                                                      503-111-2222

**CERTIFICATE OF SERVICE**

**IN THE CIRCUIT COURT FOR THE STATE OF OREGON
FOR THE COUNTY OF CLACKAMAS
Small Claims Department**

| | |
|---|---|
| JOHN SMITH, | Case No.: 18SC12345 |
| Plaintiff, | CIVIL SUBPOENA |
| v. | |
| MARK JONES, | |
| Defendant. | |

STATE OF OREGON )
                         ) ss.
County of Clackamas )

**IN THE NAME OF THE STATE OF OREGON**

TO: **FRANK JONES**

You are hereby commanded to appear in the Circuit Court for the County of Clackamas, at the Courthouse at 807 Main St., Oregon City, OR 97045 on the 15th day of March, 2018, at 1:30pm to give evidence in the above cause on behalf of Plaintiff.

Witness my hand and the seal of said Court affixed in _____ this _____ day of _____, 20\_\_\_\_.
By:_____

---

I hereby certify that I, on _____/_____/_____ in said county and state served the within subpoena on the within named person by delivering a copy thereof to said person (witness), personally and in person, and offering or giving the witness the required fees he or she is entitled to for travel and one day's attendance.


Dated: _____                          _____
                                                              Signature
                                                              Jane Williams
                                                              55 Main St., Oregon City, OR 97045
                                                              503-111-2222


**CIVIL SUBPOENA**

**IN THE CIRCUIT COURT FOR THE STATE OF OREGON
FOR THE COUNTY OF CLACKAMAS
Small Claims Department**

| | |
|---|---|
| JOHN SMITH,<br><br>       Plaintiff,<br><br>v.<br><br>MARK JONES,<br><br>       Defendant. | Case No.: 18SC12345<br><br>CIVIL SUBPOENA DUCES TECUM |

STATE OF OREGON    )
                               )  ss.
County of Clackamas   )

**IN THE NAME OF THE STATE OF OREGON**

TO: **PAYROLL RECORDS CUSTODIAN, BEST BANK, Inc.**

You are hereby commanded to produce certified copies of documents listed on the attached Addendum (and the accompanying declaration) to be potentially used as evidence in the above-named proceedings on behalf of Plaintiff, on or before 2/20/2018 at the following address: John Smith, 123 Fake St., Oregon City, OR 97045.

                               Witness my hand and the seal of said Court affixed
                               in _____ this _____ day of
                               _____, 20\_\_\_\_.
                               By:_____

---

       I hereby certify that I, on \_\_\_\_\_/_____/_____ in said county and state served the within subpoena duces tecum on the within named person by delivering a copy thereof to said person (witness), personally and in person, and offering or giving the witness the required fees he or she is entitled to under Oregon law.


Dated: _____

                                           _____
                                           Signature
                                           Jane Williams
                                           55 Main St., Oregon City, OR 97045
                                           503-111-2222


**CIVIL SUBPOENA DUCES TECUM**
Page 1 of 2

## SUBPOENA DUCES TECUM ADDENDUM

Pursuant to the attached subpoena duces tecum, you are required by order of the court to produce the following documents:

1. All monthly bank statements belonging to Mark Jones (d.o.b. 1/20/1970) for all accounts held by Best Bank, Inc. from 1/01/2017 through the present.
2. All monthly bank statements for the account ending in 7846, belonging to Frank Jones, from 1/01/2017 through the present.
3. All payroll statements for employee Doug Johnson (who worked at the branch located at 135 Commercial St., Oregon City, OR 97045) from 6/01/2016 through 9/30/2016.

### DECLARATION OF CUSTODIAN OF RECORDS
### *TO ACCOMPANY COPIES OF RECORDS*

I, _____, declare under penalty of perjury as follows:

1. I am a records custodian for _____;
2. The copy or original of the records attached to this declaration are true copies of all records which, by law, are permitted to be disclosed; and
3. That the records were prepared by the personnel of this office, or persons acting under their control, in the ordinary course of business at or near the time of the act, condition or event, which is the subject of the record.

I declare under penalty of perjury that the foregoing is true and correct.


_____
Signature


_____
Print Name
Records Custodian

# APPENDIX 2: GLOSSARY

**AFFIRMATIVE DEFENSE:** A type of defense asserted in a response in which, even if the allegations in the plaintiff's small claim are true (i.e. affirmed), the plaintiff is still not entitled to relief. For example, if the allegations in the small claim are true, but the statute of limitations has expired, the defendant would assert the affirmative defense of failing to bring a claim within the statutory period.

**APPEAL:** A request for a higher court to review the decision of a lower court. Appeals are usually not allowed in small claims cases.

**ARBITRATION:** A less formal, but usually binding proceeding in which a civil dispute is resolved by a private arbitrator, rather than a judge. Arbitration is unlikely to be an issue in a small claims case.

**BENCH TRIAL:** A trial in which there is no jury. The judge will decide all issues of law and fact. All small claims hearings are heard by a judge.

**CERTIFICATE OF SERVICE:** A document filed with the court (signed by the process server) showing that service has been completed in accordance with the rules of civil procedure.

**CLAIM FOR RELIEF:** A specific cause of action alleged in a complaint, such as a claim of negligence or a claim of racial discrimination.

**COMPLAINT:** The initial document filed by a plaintiff that begins a civil lawsuit in circuit court (referred to as a 'small claim', 'notice of small claim', or something similar in small claims court). It is a statement of how the plaintiff has been wronged by the defendant and why they should be compensated. It includes one or more claims for relief and alleges how each element of that claim has been satisfied.

**CONTEMPT OF COURT:** The offense of disobeying a court order. A judge can find a person in contempt and impose sanctions (usually a fine or other civil penalty, but on rare occasions it can include incarceration).

**CONTRACT:** Any agreement (oral or written), in which an offer has been made by one party, accepted by another, and some consideration has been given (such as money, or performance of a specific task). Breach of contract is one of the most commonly filed civil claims (whether in small claims court or regular circuit court).

**CONTRACT LAW:** One of two broad categories of civil lawsuits. All legal issues dealing with any written or oral agreement will be based on contract law.

**DEFAULT JUDGMENT:** A judgment entered against a defendant who has failed to appear after being properly served with a summons and complaint or a small claim notice.

**DEFENDANT:** A person who has been accused of wrongdoing by a plaintiff in civil court.

**DEPONENT:** The witness who is being deposed.

**DEPOSITION:** A formal interview of a witness that is recorded (usually by a court reporter transcribing the deposition).

**DISCOVERY:** The stage of a civil lawsuit wherein both parties are obligated to turn over any potential evidence that is relevant to a claim or defense.

**DISMISSAL WITHOUT PREJUDICE:** The dismissal of a plaintiff's case wherein they can refile their complaint. In other words, a judge thought the case had serious flaws, but the flaws could potentially be resolved and the case could still be refiled if the deficiencies are corrected.

**DISMISSAL WITH PREJUDICE:** The dismissal of a plaintiff's case, wherein the plaintiff cannot refile against the defendant regarding the same issue. The judge has decided that the problems with the case are so great, they cannot possibly be corrected.

**ELEMENT:** A specific aspect of a claim that must be properly alleged (and ultimately proven) to prevail on a claim for relief. A claim will normally have several elements, each of which must be proven by a preponderance of the evidence.

**EVIDENCE:** Anything that is submitted in a court proceeding to prove or disprove any claim or defense. Evidence includes (but is not limited to) oral testimony of witnesses, documents, video recordings, and material objects.

**EXHIBIT:** Any piece of evidence (other than witness testimony) that is submitted for review by a judge or jury, whether at trial or pursuant to a motion, deposition or other hearing.

**GARNISHMENT:** The legal seizing of another person's property (such as wages or funds in a bank account). Garnishment is often instituted to collect money awarded in a judgment.

**HEARING:** A proceeding before a judge in which evidence is presented and a decision is made. The decision at a hearing may affect one aspect of a case, or it may resolve the case entirely, depending on the nature of the specific hearing.

**JUDGMENT CREDITOR:** A person who has been awarded monetary damages in a civil lawsuit.

**JUDGMENT DEBTOR:** A person who has been ordered to pay a monetary damage award in a civil lawsuit.

**JURY TRIAL:** A trial in which a jury decides all factual issues. A judge will preside over the case and decide all legal issues, but the final decision regarding liability and damages will be made by the jury.

**MEDIATION:** A formal meeting between the parties and a neutral mediator in which the mediator attempts to broker a settlement that is agreeable to both sides. Unlike an arbitrator, the mediator does not have any authority to issue a decision in favor of one party. Their only purpose is to negotiate with both parties and attempt to craft a mutually agreeable settlement. In many states, parties in a small claims case must attend a mandatory mediation session and work towards resolving the issue in good faith before proceeding to a hearing.

**MOTION:** Any formal request by a party, asking the court to take a certain course of action.

**OBJECTION:** A formal protest by one party to the actions of the other party. For example, if a party seeks to submit evidence that is not in accordance with a state's rules of evidence, a party might object to its entry on the grounds that it fails to comply with said rule.

**PARTY:** A plaintiff or defendant in a civil case.

**PLAINTIFF:** A person who files a civil lawsuit against a defendant.

**PLEADINGS:** Any formal document that is filed with the court in a civil case.

**PREJUDICIAL:** In this context, prejudicial refers to how *unfairly* harmful a piece of evidence is. Evidence that would not be excluded for any other reason, can still be excluded if it will unfairly bias a jury. For example, if the jury knows a party has been convicted of a crime unrelated to the issue at hand, that could unfairly skew their impression of the party. They could seek to have that fact excluded as having more prejudicial than probative value (although there are exceptions to this particular scenario).

**PROBATIVE:** A term used to describe how strong a piece of evidence is in regards to its ability to help prove or disprove any claim or defense. How probative a piece of evidence is will often be a factor in whether or not it is admitted into the record. Evidence that has no probative value will likely be excluded.

**PROCESS SERVER:** A person who is hired by a party to deliver legal documents to someone in accordance with the rules of civil procedure.

**PRO SE:** Latin phrase meaning, "for oneself". It refers to any plaintiff or defendant that does not have an attorney. They are referred to as a *pro se* litigant or proceeding *pro se*.

**RESPONSE:** The formal reply to a small claim notice, filed by the defendant (referred to as an 'Answer' in regular circuit court). A response will usually deny the claims and either request a hearing or a jury trial.

**RULES OF CIVIL PROCEDURE:** The basic rules of civil court proceedings. Each state will have their own set of civil procedure rules (the official name of these rules will vary from state to state). These rules may or may not apply in small claims court.

**SERVICE:** The term that refers to the specific notice that pleadings have been received by an opposing party.

**SMALL CLAIMS COURT:** A division of a state court that handles claims of low economic value (the exact amount varies by state). In most states, attorneys are not allowed to represent parties in small claims court. It is intended to be a less formal and more cost-effective venue for resolving civil disputes.

**STATUTE OF LIMITATIONS:** A period set by law in which a claim for relief must be filed. For example, if the statute of limitations on a personal injury (negligence) case is two years, the plaintiff would need to file a claim for negligence within two years of the date they discovered the injury.

**STATUTES**: The codified laws of a state. The official name of these statutes will vary from state to state.

**SUBPOENA:** A command by a court or attorney requiring a person to appear for a deposition or hearing/trial.

**SUBPOENA DUCES TECUM:** A command by a court or attorney requiring a person to produce specific documents or other material objects.

**TORT LAW:** The other broad category of civil lawsuits that basically includes any type of wrongful act committed by another (other than breach of contract cases), such as battery or negligence.

**TRIAL:** A proceeding in which a final decision is made based on the merits of a case. A hearing where evidence is presented and a judge or jury finds in favor of the plaintiff or defendant.

**TRIAL COURT RULES:** More specific rules of a state that govern courtroom procedure which all county courts must follow (although all of these rules may not apply to small claims cases). The official name of these rules will vary from state to state.

**WITNESS:** Any person that provides testimony in a court proceeding. They can be a party to the litigation or any other person.

www.ingramcontent.com/pod-product-compliance
Lightning Source LLC
Chambersburg PA
CBHW020607220526
45463CB00006B/2488

Jay Barr is a lawyer practicing in Oregon who writes legal guides to help people navigate the civil court system. He has been a practicing attorney for several years and loves to help people out when they cannot afford the high cost of legal representation. Representing yourself in court is not as hard as it sounds and Mr. Barr's legal guides explain the details of civil litigation in an easy to understand manner.

Jay Barr was born and raised in Oregon and attended law school at the University of Oregon School of Law. He currently practices law in the Portland area specializing in civil litigation (Jay Barr is a pen name).

This guide offers a complete overview of how small claims courts work in most United States courthouses. It is written by a licensed attorney with years of experience counseling and advising small claims participants (lawyers are generally not allowed to represent people in small claims court). It is laid out in an easy to understand format for anyone who needs to navigate the small claims process, but is unable to afford the high cost of an attorney consultation. It includes step by step chapters that cover every major stage of a small claims case, including:

-Filing a small claim or an answer to a small claim.
-Issuing subpoenas and procuring evidence.
-Presenting evidence and examining witnesses at the small claims hearing.
-How to collect on a judgment and garnish wages or bank accounts.

Whether you are a plaintiff or a defendant, this guide will be indispensable and will ensure you have the knowledge you need to plead your case. This guide can be used in any state, but keep in mind that it provides a general overview of how litigation works in small claims court. Specific rules and procedures in your particular jurisdiction may vary.

Yes, you really can represent yourself in small claims court and win!